A Note to Pa

DK READERS is a compelling program for beginning readers, designed in conjunction with leading literacy experts, including Dr. Linda Gambrell, Director of the School of Education at Clemson University. Dr. Gambrell has served on the Board of Directors of the International Reading Association and as President of the National Reading Conference.

Beautiful illustrations and superb full-color photographs combine with engaging, easy-to-read stories to offer a fresh approach to each subject in the series. Each DK READER is guaranteed to capture a child's interest while developing his or her reading skills, general knowledge, and love of reading.

The five levels of DK READERS are aimed at different reading abilities, enabling you to choose the books that are exactly right for your child:

Pre-level 1: Learning to read
Level 1: Beginning to read
Level 2: Beginning to read alone
Level 3: Reading alone
Level 4: Proficient readers

The "normal" age at which a child begins to read can be anywhere from three to eight years old, so these levels are intended only as a general guideline.

No matter which level you select, you can be sure that you are helping your child learn to read, then read to learn!

LONDON, NEW YORK, MUNICH,
MELBOURNE, AND DELHI

Project Editor Louise Pritchard
Art Editor Jill Plank
Senior Editor Linda Esposito
Senior Art Editor
Diane Thistlethwaite
US Editor Regina Kahney
Production Melanie Dowland
Picture Researcher Andrea Sadler
Illustrator Peter Dennis

Reading Consultant
Linda Gambrell, Ph.D.

First American Edition, 2000
13 14 15 14 13 12
Published in the United States by DK Publishing
345 Hudson Street, New York, New York 10014
015-KP846-Apr/2000
Copyright © 2000 Dorling Kindersley Limited

Published in Great Britain by Dorling Kindersley Limited

Library of Congress Cataloging-in-Publication Data
Chancellor, Deborah.
   Tiger Tales / by Deborah Chancellor. --
1st American ed.
   p. cm. -- (Dorling Kindersley readers. Level 3)
   Summary: Explains the sad fate of tigers,
which are considered to be in serious danger of extinction.
   ISBN-13: 978-0-7894-5424-9 (hb)
   ISBN-13: 978-0-7894-5423-2 (pb)
   1. Tigers--Juvenile literature. 2. Endangered species--
Juvenile literature. [1. Tigers. 2. Endangered species] I. Title.
II. Series.
QL737.C23 C44 1999
599.756--dc21   99-044158

Color reproduction by Colourscan, Singapore
Printed and bound in China by L Rex Printing Co., Ltd.

The publisher would like to thank the following for their kind
permission to reproduce their images:
Key: c=centre; b=bottom; l=left; r=right; t=top
Animals Animals: Zig Leszczynski 10–11, 12–13; **A & M Shah** 14–15;
Anup Shah 21; **Ardea London Ltd: Arthus Bertrand** 38–39;
BBC Natural History Unit: John Downer 29b; Vivek Menon 20br;
Lynn Stone 47tr; Care for the Wild International: 10c; Mary Evans
Picture Library: 7tr; Oxford Scientific Films: Norbert Rosing 39tr; Planet
Earth Pictures: Tom Brakefield 13tr; Richard Matthews 22–23; Jonathan
Scott 28t.
All other images © Dorling Kindersley
For further information see: www.dkimages.com

Discover more at
www.dk.com

Contents

DK READERS

Reading Alone 3

TIGER TALES
AND BIG CAT STORIES

Written by Deborah Chancellor

DK Publishing

Tigers in danger

Beneath the tall trees of a dark rainforest in Malaysia, a tiger crouched in the gloom. He did not recognize the sound of traffic, a soft hum in the distance. He had strayed beyond his usual hunting ground and was trying to get back to a familiar part of the forest. As he walked on, the noise grew louder.

Suddenly, the leafy cover of the trees disappeared and the glare of bright sunlight dazzled the tiger. He broke out from the shadows and blundered onto a busy highway. The road stretched along the borders of the tiger's forest. The frightened tiger did not stop in his tracks or turn back to safety.

Instead, he ran onto the road, straight into the traffic. There was a screech of brakes as a bus slammed into the tiger, killing him instantly.

The flow of cars and trucks slowed against a din of hooting horns. A crowd gathered to watch as the dead animal was moved to the side of the road.

In the next 24 hours, the tiger's body was gutted – not by hungry animals, but by greedy people. The tiger's claws and teeth, and even his whiskers, vanished.

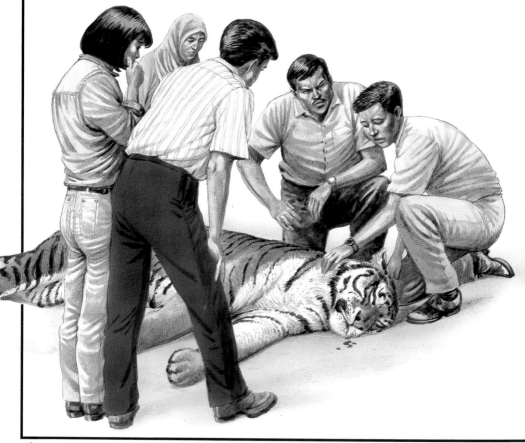

This happened because the thieves could sell the parts of the tiger's body. The parts are used in traditional Chinese medicine. This form of medicine makes remedies from animals and plants. It has been used in China for thousands of years.

Traditional Chinese drugstore

Traditional medicine

Most parts of a tiger are used in Chinese medicine. The whiskers are said to relieve toothache and the brain is thought to cure laziness.

In China, as in most countries, buying and selling tigers is against the law. But tigers are still hunted, mainly because they can be sold to the Chinese medicine trade for a lot of money. At least one tiger is killed every day. The world's tigers are now in serious danger.

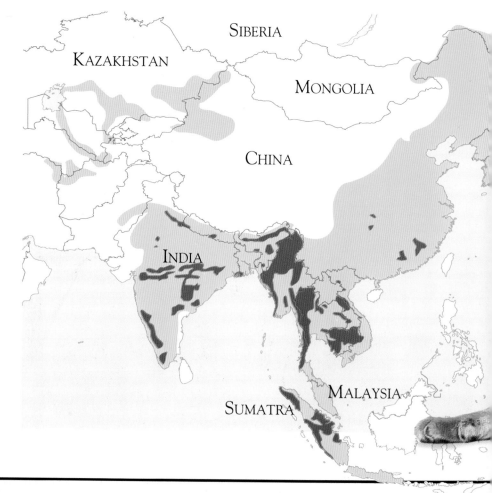

At the start of the 20th century, there were about 100,000 tigers in the world. Now there are only about 6,000 left. They roam the forests and plains of Asia, from the far east of Russia to western India, and from Sumatra in the south to China in the north.

RUSSIA

Where tigers may be found today.

Where tigers lived 100 years ago.

Tigers are magnificent creatures. It would be very sad if they became extinct (died out completely). Many people are working hard to make sure the tiger does not become extinct.

Care for the Wild International is a British group that sets up safe places, called reserves, for tigers to live in. These reserves are in the jungle, where the tigers live naturally.

The group recently rescued some tigers in Cambodia.

Two young cubs were snatched from their den while their mother was out hunting. The kidnappers wanted to sell them in Vietnam, just across the border.

Luckily, the cubs were discovered just in time by wildlife protection officers. They took the cubs away from the kidnappers and rushed them to an animal rescue center.

Tiger cub diet

Cubs drink their mother's milk when they are born. When they are about two months old, their mother starts to bring them meat.

Care for the Wild International sent two veterinarians – animal doctors – to care for the tiger cubs. The cubs were thin and their legs were badly bent from rickets, a disease caused by a bad diet.

The cubs were called Map and Tomi, common names in the local language.

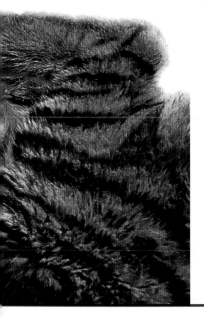

They were gradually nursed back to health. By the age of six months they were both eating about two and a half pounds (one kg) of meat every day.

In the wild, tiger cubs stay with their mother for two years. At about five months old, they start to learn how to find food. They "help" their mother by frightening small animals out of the bush for her to pounce on.

From seven months, tiger cubs go everywhere with their mother, learning how to hunt by watching her in action.

Sadly, Map and Tomi can never return to the jungle. No human can teach them the skills their mother would have taught them. Care for the Wild International is making a reserve specially for them, where they will have as much freedom as possible. They will enjoy the company of a tigress called K'mik, who is coming to live with them.

Tiger terror

One quiet January evening, a young man was washing some clothes in his back yard. His home was just outside a national park in Thailand. Suddenly, the calm was broken by the cries of frightened deer in the woods nearby. Afraid for his  own life, the man ran for the safety of his house. But he never made it.

With a sharp snap of branches, a six-foot-long tiger leaped at him from the bushes. It knocked him to the ground and sank its teeth into his hand.

Then the massive animal began to
drag him toward the trees. Bleeding and
in pain, the man struggled and shouted
for help. A friend heard his cries and
ran to the rescue. But the tiger turned
and attacked him too.

The screams of both men raised the alarm. Help arrived, this time from armed park officers, who fired their rifles into the air. This was enough to scare the tiger back into the forest.

Amazingly, the two men lived to tell the tale, with only small injuries.

Eyesight

Like other big cats, tigers can see well in the dark. They hunt at dawn, dusk, or by night, when they can surprise their prey.

True stories like this one
are frightening, but tigers do
not usually attack people. If a
tiger is ill or injured, it is easier
for it to kill a human than other prey.
The tiger that attacked the young men
was probably old and starving. It was
lucky to survive its contact with humans
and escape back to the jungle.

Healthy tigers can kill animals that weigh more than they do. Even young rhinos and elephants are not safe. Tigers can eat more than 65 pounds (30 kgs) of meat in one night, but they may need a big meal like this only once or twice a week. However, only one out of 15 hunts is successful.

Tigers usually hunt deer, wild boar, and other medium-sized forest animals. Between hunts, they snack on crabs, turtles, fish, and lizards, and sometimes locusts and fruit. They eat grass and mud to help them digest their food.

Tiger teeth
A tiger's teeth are perfect for catching, killing, and eating. Some teeth stab and grip, some bite and slice, and others grind.

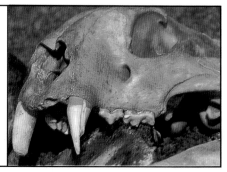

Tigers do not choose to clash with humans. The problem is that people bring their world too close to the tigers' forest home.

Over the last 100 years, large areas of the world's rainforests have been destroyed to make way for roads, towns, and industries. This cuts back the amount of forest for tigers to live in and reduces the number of animals for tigers to prey on. The result is that hungry tigers are forced to hunt closer to people's homes and jobs to find food. This can lead to disaster.

Territory

Tigers mark out a patch of the forest to hunt in and defend as their own. This is their territory. A territory can be hundreds of square miles (kilometers).

One part of the world where a large area of rainforest has disappeared is southern Sumatra, in Indonesia. Trees are now being planted here to help the forest grow back again. This action is called reforestation.

People working on the project are dangerously close to tigers. One day, a tiger leaped out from the forest. It killed three people and mauled three more. After that, many workers refused to return to their jobs. Sadly, the tiger had scared away people who were helping it. But luckily, the reforestation continues.

Camouflage

A tiger's striped coat helps it to hide in the forest. The ability of animals to blend in with their background is called camouflage.

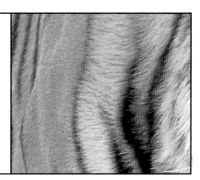

Set us free

It can be upsetting to see a proud lion in a zoo, pacing back and forth inside a cage. He will probably never set foot in his natural habitat, the open spaces of the African grasslands.

Some people work hard to return lions to their natural habitat. The lions must be young and not too used to human contact. They must be able to learn the skills they need to survive on their own in the wild.

Gareth Patterson is well known for his work with lions in southern Africa. He has spent years trying to improve their living conditions in captivity and helping some back to the wild. His stories about these lions tell us about the dangers facing lions in Africa today.

This is a story of a lioness and her three cubs that Gareth helped to save.

Early one morning, the lioness woke with her cubs beside her. They were just five days old and completely helpless. They could barely crawl and would not even open their eyes for another week.

Just before the cubs were born, the lioness had left the family group she lived with, called a pride. For the first six weeks of their lives, her tiny cubs would be safer away from the rough male members of the pride.

Usually she hunted zebra or gazelle with the help of her pride mates. But hunting alone, she could kill only a cow on a nearby farm. Later that day, the angry farmer shot her dead.

Luckily, people discovered the motherless cubs. They named the male cub Batian after M'batian, a nearby mountain. The two female cubs were named Rafiki and Furaha, meaning "friend" and "joy" in the local language.

The cubs were given to a man named George Adamson, who was well known for returning lions to the wild. But not long afterward, Adamson was killed by people who made money by killing and selling the bodies of lions illegally. Gareth Patterson took over the care of the three cubs.

George Adamson

George was made famous in the 1960s by the film *Born Free*. It was about him and his wife, Joy, and their work with lions in Africa.

Gareth took Batian, Rafiki, and Furaha to the Tuli bushlands in southern Africa. One day Batian roamed away from his sisters in search of a mate. He followed a group of lionesses and found himself far away from home.

Batian was hungry and alone in an unfamiliar land. As the sun set, he heard the distant noise of hyenas and jackals feeding. His ears twitched, picking up the direction of the sound. Perhaps the hyenas would leave some meat. Then he could have an easy meal.

Like all lions, Batian's sense of smell was far better than a human's. Soon he picked up the scent of a dead animal. He followed his nose and found a dead donkey chained to a tree. The sounds of hyenas and jackals were coming from a loudspeaker. Batian had been lured into a trap.

A shot rang out and Batian fell to the ground, killed by a bullet to his head. He was only three years old.

A professional hunter and an American tourist were at the scene of Batian's murder. They probably shot Batian to sell his skin. This is against the law. The owner and manager of the ranch where Batian was killed were fined. But crimes like this are common and the punishments do not work. Three years later, another young lion was killed in the same way on the same ranch.

Lion alert

The Serengeti in Africa is the world's most famous national park. It stretches over 5,600 square miles (14,500 square kilometers) of Tanzania and is home to around 3,000 lions. Lions were once common all over Africa, but now there are only about 100,000 left. Most live in reserves like the Serengeti, where people can see them but where they are safe from human hunters.

In February 1994, a group of tourists were watching wildlife in the Serengeti from a hot-air balloon. Suddenly, they saw a lion thrashing around, struggling to stand. The balloon pilot called the Serengeti's chief veterinarian, who examined the distressed animal. The lion was seriously ill. It died that night.

Over the next few weeks, 11 more lions died in a similar way. The next year, 1,000 of the Serengeti's 3,000 lions were wiped out.

The illness spread to the Masai Mara reserve in Kenya, killing a third of the lions there. Something had to be done, and fast, to stop the illness from spreading and endangering all the lions.

Food for the pride

Lions often hunt large prey, such as buffalo, for the whole pride. The big males take most. Sometimes there is nothing left for the cubs.

Scientists discovered that the lions were dying from a virus normally found in dogs. They caught it from the hyenas and jackals that shared their kills.

The hyenas and jackals had not started the outbreak. They had been infected by the guard dogs kept by local people to protect their cattle.

The solution was simple: stamp out the virus where it first appeared. Thousands of guard dogs around the Serengeti were given injections to stop them from getting, and then passing on, the disease.

The project was called Project Life Lion. Money and help poured in from people and wildlife organizations around the world.

After a long program of dog vaccinations, it now looks as if Project Life Lion has worked. The Serengeti lions are at last out of serious danger.

The beast of Exmoor

One night in 1983, some farmers in Exmoor, a region in southwest England, had a nasty surprise. Something had savagely attacked and killed 80 of their lambs and sheep. From the unusual claw marks and footprints, it looked like a large wild cat was to blame. Whatever it was had ripped the sheep's throats in the same way that a big cat, such as a puma, would attack its prey.

Since then, many more farm animals in the area have become victims of the mysterious killer.

No big cats live naturally in this part of England. Some experts believe that a puma may have escaped from a zoo and adapted to life in the wild. The local landscape is a mixture of rocky, wooded, and open spaces – perfect for pumas.

A number of people claim to have seen the elusive "beast of Exmoor." They tell of an animal that looks like a cat, about four feet (1.25 meters) long and two feet (60 centimeters) tall, with a long tail and a dark coat.

A pet-shop owner named David Smith, from a town near Exmoor, swears he came face-to-face with the animal when he was out hunting one day. He had sent his dog into the bushes to flush out some rabbits.

Suddenly, a puma-like creature emerged
from the brushwood and bounded past
him into some marshland. David
decided not to shoot the animal.

"I was only there for rabbits and I
thought I should spare its life," he said.

No one knows to this day what
animal is responsible for the attacks.

The world's big cats

We do not know much about the secretive life of the "beast of Exmoor," but we know about the rest of the world's big cats. There are eight species of big cat – the lion, tiger, jaguar, leopard, snow leopard, clouded leopard, puma, and cheetah. All of them are carnivores, or meat eaters.

The tiger, jaguar, puma, and leopard ambush their prey. The lion and cheetah chase their prey.

Cheetah   Puma   Jaguar

The markings on big cats keep them hidden, or camouflaged, when they hunt. The tiger has stripes and the jaguar, cheetah, and leopard have spots. Lions and pumas have plain coats, but their cubs have spots to hide them from animals that may kill them.

Clouded leopard

Snow leopard

Leopard   *Tiger*   *Lion*

Glossary

Camouflage
The color patterns or body shapes that help to hide an animal in its surroundings.

Carnivore
An animal that eats mainly meat. It has specially shaped teeth to enable it to kill and eat its food.

Conservation
The management of the Earth's resources, to protect the natural world.

Diet
The kind of food an animal usually eats.

Extinct
Describes a species of animal that has died out, or has not been seen for at least 50 years.

Habitat
The place where an animal lives, for example, a jungle or a desert

Jungle
An area of land covered in tangled trees and bushes, such as a rainforest.

National park
An area of countryside, protected because of its natural beauty and wildlife.

Poacher
A person who hunts and kills animals against the law.

Prey
An animal that is caught and eaten by another animal.

Pride
A family group of lions. A pride consists of three or four males and 10 or more females and cubs.

Rainforest
A tropical forest that has heavy rainfall. Rainforests are rich in plant and animal life.

Reforestation
Planting trees to replace those cut down in a forest.

Reserve
A protected area of land that provides animals with a safe place to live.

Rickets
A disease that makes the bones go soft, due to a lack of certain vitamins.

Scavenge
To feed on the leftovers of an animal that was killed and fed on by another animal.

Senses
Animals find out about their surroundings with their senses. The five senses are sight, hearing, smell, taste, and touch.

Species
A type of animal or plant. Any male and female member of the same species can breed together.

Territory
An area of land in which an animal or group of animals hunts, breeds, and defends against other animals.

Virus
An illness or sickness that can spread quickly from animal to animal.